# SPRING OF THE MUSES

## *The Poetry of Music, Art and Dance*

Edited by Deborah Gaye

AVALANCHE BOOKS

Published in Great Britain by Avalanche Books England 2019

Printed by SRP, England



British Library Cataloguing in Publication Data. A catalogue record for this book is available from the British Library.

ISBN: 978 1 874392 06 4

# INTRODUCTION

"Spring of the Muses" is a celebration of poetry, art, music and dance and it brings together a vibrant collection of poems upon the theme.

*"A poem is a speaking picture, a picture a silent poem"*

Simonides of Ceos

The histories of art and poetry and of poetry and music have always been creatively intertwined. It is thought that the earliest expressions of poetry were either recited or sung.
This anthology of poetry and short prose explores that rich tradition and in so doing reveals how different art forms can combine to inspire, enrich and energise each other.

*"Poetry is the music of the soul, and above all of great and feeling souls"*

Voltaire

*"Dance is the hidden language of the soul of the body"*

Martha Graham

## *Contents*

## THE SONG

I would write words
For the song you tried to teach me
Humming it in snatches
Saying *It goes something like this*
*Which is all I can remember,*
Since when your forgetfulness
Has been a gift as precious
As that summer afternoon,
Its long grass lying
Printed where we lay,
Our laughter a notation
Carrying on the breeze
In search of what might still
Return to us, reclaimed
And set to music
With such words as these

*John Mole*

## THE INSOLUBLE HARMONIES OF COLOUR

The old man sat down against a stump of reflection and began to strip the bark from his torment with a sharp intake of breath.

'I have,' he thought, 'always expected my dour palette to yield a colour bright enough to lead me, with no consideration of the canvas to which I may have applied it. My brushes were the rocks of my ignorance which I did not learn to use with delicacy, and my pigment I hid jealously beneath my contempt for the opinions of others. Now I am alone, and my paint has hardened beyond use.'

As he softly easeled his head on hands tangled like the knuckled roots of an ancient tree, he heard a chorus of sheep bleating a ruminating song while they ambled slowly towards him.

The old man recognised the song at once, and raised his gaze to meet the bearded face of a venerable bellwether.

'It's a simple song,' offered the bellwether as a greeting, with a smile. 'We chew, we sleep, we sing, we amble. The colours of our life are few and muted.'

'Yet you paint so beautifully with them,' replied the old man, moved and quieted by the unaffected honesty of the ram. 'I could not match your mastery.'

'We paint what we are able, old man, we make no study of our inability. Our song does not change with expectation.'

'Even so, do you never wish for more than you have?' asked the old man, keenly, trying for a moment to comprehend the absence of desire.
'More suns? More grass? More sleep? More song? How would we profit from such a wish, or even the hope that such a wish may be granted? Shrugged the bellwether with a cordial chuckle.
'I have always wished for more,' sighed the old man, apologetically. 'My life has been spent in the pursuit of a formula which would multiply my desires and secure my success. I realise now that my efforts have been wasted, I have not in all my searching found the words to my song.'
The bellwether looked thoughtfully at the old man and attempted to understand the nagging root of his anguish.
'We are sheep,' he began, following a few moments of puzzled headscratching and another good natured shrug, 'we have no comprehension of the meaning of your words.'
'My words are simple. I am a man, and as all men, I burned with the desire to succeed. To be better than all other men, to confront my peers with my finery, to arm myself with riches, to cultivate envy among my fellows.'
'To what purpose?' begged the baffled ram.
The old man let loose a long sigh and looked hard into a hazy distance for a reply.
'To be accepted,' he mused at last, 'to be recognised as one of my flock. To follow what was expected of me. To be an example of conformity and to sing a song which everyone knew.'

‘You are too clever for me, old man. We sheep are uncomplicated beasts; we greet the sun in the morning, meander over meadows in song, chew the sweet clover and frolic in silvery streams. If we were intelligent animals, maybe we, too, would cultivate desires and strive for success, but as it is, we can only marvel at the strange magic of your words and carry on singing.’
And as the swelling sun shone like saffron on water hills, the old man searched the stretched and pine-selvaged skyline for a cooling shower of unformed replies, while the bellwether ambled away with his bleating number toward a fresh green pasture, chewing and frolicking and singing the same song they had always sung.

*Chris Tutton*

## FLOWERS, BLANKETS

*for Anya Gallacio & her installation at Lindisfarne Castle*

Wrapped in a silence that asks for nothing
and is given everything
we kneel, enchanted
taken home
to the kiss of wool and all light's colours

Hungry tongues soothed with weld
and indigo, marigold
madder *which hath an opening quality,*
*and afterwards to bind and strengthen*

Where outside is inside
we are bound and strengthened
by her dyeing, gathered by the plants
we gather
armfuls of more than we need
to see us onward, through

*Linda France*

* *which hath...* from John Gerard's *Herball, 1597*

## BACKGROUND MUSIC

You may be in a café reading when,
after the intro, Billie Holliday
and *Easy Living* lure you out of Walden
and swing you in a trance out of the café.

You may be watching Shaun Evans as Morse
mostly to marvel at the mimicry
of his body language, so like John Thaw's,
when you're torn away, this time by Puccini,

away from the spires of Oxford to fall,
to fall as Tosca falls, defences fall,
that your heart breaks open a dungeon door

and griefs like prisoners crouched on the floor
bestir themselves and infant griefs like dolls
sleep through a bell that tolls and tolls and tolls.

*Mimi Khalvati*

## SCHUMANN AT MIDNIGHT

He sits at the piano, where a sliver
Of yellow light
Winds through a maze of shadows; she, on covers
Cool and white.
The bedroom floods with music, and she shivers.

His shoulders square against her are a wall
She cannot scale.
But from behind his stiff-backed silence spills
A different tale,
One she knows the movements of too well.

Here are the high, fine, thrilling notes, cross-grained
Against the dark,
And here, the thread that binds them and explains
The chords that part
Far off and found again; part, and are found again.

*Katrina Porteous*

## HARMONY

Though we may have different words
for love and prayer
it's the same dawn chorus
that sweetens our mornings,
the same moon
that butters our midnight gardens
with its light.
And, though we may not know it,
In the evenings
when onions and spices
are sizzling in their frying pans
and lentils are softening in the pot,
the steamy songs of our kitchens
sneak out to find each other,
fuse and tangle over our roof tops
and sing.

*Gaia Holmes*

## KEELBY 1966

This song of Sunday afternoon
laments tax and divorce.
But you flicked dials to lend the tune
all your transistor's force.
The dark hair wavered by your arms
brief sun was all we knew
as we cut back on the baked path
by which the barley blew.

*Alison Brackenbury*

*The song is* 'Sunny Afternoon' *by The Kinks*

## ON HOLD

A sudden music from the phone
spills over me, by someone who
you met. If he still lived, like you,
would he hum, rock, his eyes half-closed,
or fume, like us, fifth in the queue?

*Alison Brackenbury*

## ORIEL MONS PICTURE GALLERY, SUNDAY AFTERNOON

Stepping back, I tread accidentally on a white plimsoll
looking down I spot new shoes, looking up
to apologise our eyes lock and in that moment

past loves and lives flash by as if in a dream
about drowning and for a second, I understand
about love and all that word entails. And now

a woman who has lived through much stands
mesmerised
by paintings and a stranger. For this brief whisper almost
there is happiness and there is clarity and, in this clarity,

he moves on. Subtle blues, mauves, greens of an artist's
perception
capture another vision and I hope I haven't left a mark
on this shoe
for a while, right-footed plimsoll now carries my weight.

*Wendy French*

## HIS LOVER'S ARM

*On Duncan Grant's murals in Lincoln Cathedral dedicated to the patron saint of the woollen industry, St Blaize*

I read they locked your lust away for years,
the chantry a broom cupboard where only
the sun could eye the mural pastels.

You were sixty, he was half your age
when he posed for the sketches of shearers.
Your brush speaks on his arm.

A mandora of light envelops the Good Shepherd
who has his face, his splendid limbs;
the ones you traced with your deft fingers.

It's more than plain that this anatomy
was something that was never
learned from books. St Blaize

leans from a roundel on the side wall.
They said he had your face
which leered at his Christ.

The sheared sheep are blue,
and look bereft. He left
before you made
the final touches.

*Kathryn Daszkievicz*

## ADORATION OF THE KINGS

*after Breughel*

Everything looks rough-hewn and doltish
and has done so since my eyes
began to betray me unreliably now I peer
through thick blue saucers of glass

yet I feel how these strangers have stirred us
this one with the pinched face of a carpenter
more than king though the bold red
of his sleeves and collar and the aureate bowl

his fingers dandle appear rich indeed
and so wholly out of place in our stable-yard
where we've found this squalling child
reluctant and bollock-naked as far as I can see

then the older one with his lank grey hair
stoops as if to show off his ermine trim
and his extraordinarily long pink sleeves
(I see them more clearly than anything else)

positioning his hat and mace in the dirt
to offer a gift of something I can't make out
beside me the black skin and sharp leather smell
of a third who holds his elaborate gift

of green and yellow – it must be jade and gold
yet it smells sweetly of spices to me
a sort of sweetness like nothing I've known
and I can tell you I'm good with odours

even better with my ears which are sharp enough
to follow the munching commentary
of the ass in the byre and the shift of the crowd
and the hiss of the doltish Piet with his lips

to the father's ear informing him I suppose
what everyone here knows of the difference
in their ages and the forbidding signs
from the fractious boy even the fact this child

cannot possibly be his – shit-for-brains Piet
in his green snood has never been one to look
past the obvious not someone to let gossip
go abegging yet hasn't the mother's face

turned now half-obscured as if she wants us
to believe there's something in all this
not the sighted nor the blind might fathom
a secret that she and her foreign friends are keeping

*Martyn Crucefix*

## VENUS AND MARS

Two Sèvres porcelain vases
covered in gold leaf,
nude nymphs
cascading down the sides.

Shipped in the nineteenth century
from Paris to Cartagena,
a gift such as Louis XV
gave to Mme de Pompadour,
they travelled by mule
over the cordilleras
from Honda in Tolima, to Bogotá.

They bobbed hundreds of miles,
mouths open,
lurching over the mountains.
And not a crack, not a chip,
just here and there,
the loss of some leaf.
Each individually signed.

For the white and pink and blue
empty amphoras tossed about on
the new continent,
for water un-poured, poured.
For heat and mosquitoes,
mud and freezing nights
around a brazier.

For a patina of mist
burnt off after dawn,
for the watchmen on love's journey
and the sheer lunacy of it all,
I have instead,
these lines, *amor.*

*Isabel Bermudez*

## A ROTHKO MORNING

*after* The Seagram Murals *by Mark Rothko*

I wake up on a ridge high above
the reach of early sun.
I stare down at morning
flushed violet by night.
Wrens and finches cease
pre-dawn chittering.
Quiet wraps me.

The earth warms.
Sharp frost snaps.
Mauve rises from fissures,
slides across my tongue
like a satin ball-gown
slipping over shoulders.

Below, an orchestra tunes
to the A flat of a valley
released from night.
Day comes to claim me.

*Kaye Lee*

## SCOTTISH BARONIAL

When I think of it now, it opens like a music box,
That dank castle overlooking the estuary.
Up an overgrown cart-track we found it at dusk,
Rooks in narrow turrets, its slates awry.

There was talk of a benefits scam. A rag-bag
Assortment of travellers, skunk-dealers, tree-dwellers,
healers
With crystals and feathers, holed up, burning candles
And sometimes the furniture, under its lofty ceilings.

And there was your daughter, pale, dreadlocked; and the
first of six
Dusty grand pianos; and one after another,
You threw those great rooms open, and every one
Flooded with music of a different colour;

Those poor, out-of-tune, rattling pianos –
Fin-de-siècle exiles of concert-hall or ballroom
Long fallen silent before the vanishing tide
Out on the mud-flats – singing, one last time.

*Katrina Porteous*

## FERMENTED CHERRIES

The Fado rolls out, washing over me. It's a salt-weighted tide that ebbs and rises above the listeners' heads. The vocalist leans on the humid air, lungs hauling in breath and pushing it out as song.

I stand in the doorway, held steady by the sound and by a burst of heat from the kitchen where sardines roast in rows.

I can see him sitting near the bar, a glass of ruby liquid cradled in one hand. The light catches on his hair and settle in crows' feet like sediment.

It's more than a decade since we left, since he called my mother a whore within my hearing, since I heard him call me a whore's wretched beastling. She'd endured seven years of his outrage since I took root, but this was the first time he'd thought to insult me.

It was enough to make her pack our scant possessions and fly us far away.

Last time I saw him I was small enough to clamber on his knee. Now, if he stood, I'd tower over him. He half smiles into the Fado song, soaking up its sweet melancholy.

I don't wait for a break in the music. I shore up my courage and wade across the room, treading shadows until I'm by his side. Then I crouch low and sudden so that he startles and port sloshes in his glass – a small crimson tsunami.

"Avô," I say, using the Portuguese word for grandfather. It tastes strange in my mouth – like a

mixture of brine and fermented cherries. "Avô, I'm here to tell you that your daughter has died."
And I watch the sea brim in his eyes.

*Judy Darley*

## POSTCARDS

I burned them, you know.
The parrot's cocked eye
the note where you wished me
'green days'. I burned too
the one with the man with the beautiful hands,
so vain; so precisely like you.

*Alison Brackenbury*

## LIGHT

One spring dawn, I heard someone outside singing the most beautiful song I had ever heard in a language which sounded as if it came from another time. I got up and pulled back the curtains. Through the window, I could see a youth walking across the dewy field at the back of our house. Although I was afraid, I couldn't resist waving. With a gesture he invited me to come out and join him, and I knew he would not mock me if I sang along with him, although I had no idea what it was I was meant to sing.

*Ian Seed*

## D. 959

Late style's always relative,
but thirty-one! Beethoven's
dead and he has only months,
and there's so much to be said.
What to do but carry on,
reinvent sonata form?

Snape on a soft June evening:
Brendel plays. Close to the stage,
I watch hands on keys and catch
that famous tuneless humming,
while the first movement unfolds
a contour map of its world.

The andantino begins,
merging purpose and caress,
as glanced-at pain and regret
fragment into *Sturm und Drang*;
its theme returns transfigured
by sly quavering repeats.

Schubert pretends that all's well
in his rondo finale.
He lies; and he knows he lies,
for things slide to the minor
as the rumbling storm returns,
yet his spirit's undaunted.

Like Prospero, he sums up,
imploring us for release,
which we unstintingly grant;
I hear, as the record ends
in another time and place,
these hands join in the applause.

*Neil Powell*

## ON THE SHORELINE

I have come to love the fisherman's upturned boat,
sea-weed darkened. I walk on the shingle.
A tree without branches grows on the shoreline –
further inland the dog-rose.

I've forgotten a truth I once knew –
at a harp without strings the harpist flounders.
The music is there in the ache of my body,
in words beyond this night.

*Wendy French*

## THE GHOST DANCE

In the morning, I folded you onto my
pillow. Whisper-kissed your blush skin

soft, burrowed for rhymes in the oasis of
your hair, remembered when it was easy,

like listening to Sidney Bechet in the
summer afternoon sun of your fingers.

*Chris Tutton*

# CELLO SUITES

i

*Rostropovich, King's College Chapel*

It was there, between us, palpable –
wrapped in blue air, outlined almost
in gold, like dust from the wings
of an angel (if such things existed),
damming the music in its flood
like a heavenly blood-clot, clenching
ventricles, nailing the heart
to the great ribbed vaulting (this landbound
ark) and one of us crying, it's not
clear who, as if for joy, or loss; and the dust
stirs briefly like the tremors of love
satisfied, or of grief. And it's gone

and you catch yourself thinking
*this is the moment; this mystery,*
*this is where history starts.*
And somewhere else a wing unfurls;
here, you're caught up once
and lifted, shipwrecked, drowning.

ii

*Steven Isserlis, Exeter Cathedral*

After all those words
a river of uncluttered notes.
'I'd like to be voiceless now
for days,' you whisper.

Something beyond language
opens its wings inside us;
bears us out streaming
into blue silence.

*Roselle Angwin*

## LE ISOLA MAGGIORE

You've fallen in love with this shuttered life:
            its elegiac pace, the way
wooden slats stripe the marbled, bedroom tiles.

You return here frequently, like the swifts
        who circle the palazzo,
ruined tower and crumbling banquet halls.

You show me the Madonna and Child,
        glowing with lapis lazuli, gold leaf;
a fresco of St Sebastian, (said to keep the plague at bay),

pierced by seven arrow heads. We dip
        our feet into the lake. Blood-warm to the touch,
it's silting up, like the weathered inhabitants.

Lake Trasimeno lies on a seismic fault:
        the earth's plates, like Roman gods
shifting beneath its weight. A white egret

makes a low, majestic flight towards the pines.
        Once the ferry leaves, the island's silent,
like *La Chiesa del Buon Morto,* padlocked for the night.

*Anne Caldwell*

## LYTTON (i)
## Portrait
### (from The Carrington Sketches)

She mixes a warmer red to paint his beard.
Love guides the strokes. He’s in the green armchair

and she is glad to find him there, unmoved
when she awakes. She talks to him

in the passionate ink of her journal
as if he’s God. *You seem so wise*

*and very coldly old.* So she foresees
the misery.

Later she’ll paint the mill they share at Tidmarsh:
its sloping roofs will glow with that same squirrel red.

She’ll paint the river which flows underneath
the tunnel mouth a widening O of black.

*Kathryn Daszkievicz*

## OPHELIA DROWNING IN THE TATE

*after Millais*

Once I picked flowers:
bluebell, flax and celandine,
held each one like a tiny hand
spread out in asking.

Through the water meadows:
crowfoot, flag and violet,
I gathered them in a posy,
as if walking to a wedding.

Now, as you look from
your hide outside the wall,
you see me ever drowning;
fitting to the water like my own cast.

You watch me
as I shake the elements,
split the join from air to water,
water back to air.

And, as forever
life shifts round me,
forever is renewed and drained away,
I see your eyes;

blue, green, brown,
the colours of a landscape;
they haunt me from the bank:
bluebell, flax and celandine,
crowfoot, flag and violet.

*Simon Williams*

## THE ARTIST AS A CHILD

*after Federico Garcia Lorca*

Everything that happens must happen here,
he thought, within the confines of the page.
Marshal your pencils then, master your fear.
Start with the sky, take the blue to the edge.

Leave no patch of white, no eye, no space.
Every block that is coloured in permits
relief and progress up the rooftop staircase,
flag by flag, to the wrought-iron parapets.

What is the void but love between two walls?
Don't fudge the corners where the angles dovetail.
Neither love nor fear can be drawn to scale.

Limbs that won't fit in if the trunk's too tall –
abbreviate. Let fortune be your draughtsman.
Look to your moon, black moon, your red-half-curtain.

*Mimi Khalvati*

## CLAPPERBOARDS

*after Cape Cod Morning by Edward Hopper*

It took twenty years or more
before the trees gave up their souls
and bodies to the woodcutter.

Summer, autumn, winter and spring
seasoned the sappy wood before
they cut it into boards

to build the house and paint it white,
catching the light which seemed to fall
sideways on her waiting face

as she stood for hours in the place
where she could watch
the ever-empty sea.

*Alwyn Marriage*

## REMEDIOS VARO PAINTS

Remedios paints the measure of a dream.
She paints it into the forest;
an armillary constructed purely of light,
a hovering astrolabe, unearthly
as the gasping stars.

She paints in a tower inhabited
by two of her starwatchers
distinct in the background, but the foreground
is what is holding their eyes.

They reconnaitre with a waxing gibbous
moon on the lake
while waning sun, out of their sightline
is held up like an apple
rose tinted in bare boughs.

Remedios is painting bright bridleways
she hangs over the water,
chalky and luminous
and circular as desire.

They are spinning slowly on one axis,
in time with the turning of planets
magnetic as cosmos flowers
to night-flying eyes of winged things
out and about in her paintbrush.

From its shivering dance
comes a map of untameable worlds
and art, of course, art
brings the unknown close.

Here is a vision bold enough
to conquer the stranglehold of time,
spinning the kind of enlightenment
her watchers absorb
through their skins.

Solutions to problems tumble from them
in waves of a new language
Remedios paints onto their tongues.
Here is the creative spark,
the hunger for renewal.

*Susan Taylor*

## WAITING

*after Rabindranath Tagore*

We sit,
we wait
like shimmering birds
on a telephone wire.

Anonymous
in our sitting
and our waiting;

sari-wrapped:
purple, blue,
billowing rows
of eternity.

Anonymous
in our fluidity,
in our patience,
in our sisterhood;

we sit,
we wait
in the evening
like jewels in the dust.

Pensive,
we are what we know,
universal.
We are women.

*Debjani Chatterjee*

## BLUE MOON HAIKU

Blue moon, your curved smile
and stance are the Flute Player’s.
Both stealers of hearts.

*Debjani Chatterjee*

## DANCE

On the floor
near where Shiva dances
a woman's hair
breaks gold-tipped
wave upon wave

beyond the glass
the cedar stretches
towards translucent
January blue

and beyond the tree
the heather moor
just

is

*Roselle Angwin*

## STORM SMELL

*after* Tornado *by Francis Alys*

There must be a smell here –
ravaged earth, bloodied trees,
shreddings of summer grass –
but the roar from giant
rotating corkscrews
of ochre, black, bridal-veil white
shuts down my olfactory
nerves, turns me into a funnel
of ears, eyes and skin
teased by a silk shroud
of dust before the smarting
scrape of spiked rain.
One day I'll catch
a tornado, inhale
the odour
of a still
heart.

*Kaye Lee*

## WILD GARLIC

*through the sandstone bridge,* she said
*flows the river Spey;*
*where the wild garlic grows*
*won't you come and play?*

*let's play tickle trout,* she sighed
whispering like the river
*I would* said I, *but...can't be late*
*back home for me dinner*

yet homewards over the mossy wall
beneath the weeping beech
*Why not stay and rest awhile*
her blue eyes did beseech

her blue eyes did beseech, and she
handed me some fruit,
a granny smith that began to blush
at all her talk of juice

all her talk of juice was like
a philtre drunk at bed,
it made me dream a freckled trout
was standing there instead

a freckled trout standing there,
androgynous, divine,
singing of the liquid bliss
together we would find

*together we would find,* she sang
fluttering her gills,
*the love that breathes in silver streams,*
*a love for which you'd kill*

*a love for which you'd kill* – I mused
it filled me full of doubt,
sang beneath the weeping beech
by a brown and freckled trout

a brown and freckled trout, she was
in a sequin dress
that shimmered round her swinging hips
in whisperings of bliss

whisperings of bliss that told
how – on the other side
things are more than they seem
girl   river   trout

*Mark Gwynne Jones*

## SHEELA NA GIG, ST MICHAELS, OXFORD

Her legs are parted to the day.
They prised her from the tower wall
before car fumes ate her away.

She shows no face. She bares no breast.
The priests claim she is not obscene:
a builder's warning against lust.

I laugh. I brush them off. I stare
into the black line of her slit.
How deep lips dance, how bare, how bare.

*Alison Brackenbury*

## TULIPOMANIA

*after Rory McEwen's watercolours on vellum*

What binds you is a puzzle,
nub ruched in chlorophyll;
vellum high-drama – those push-me
pull-you strokes I must pluck out
my eyes to elucidate.

*Old English Striped Tulip 'Sam Barlow'*

Flamingoed half to death,
queer, alcoholic pink,
I accuse you a keeper of secrets,
kisser of bruised lips,
inarticulate with thirst.

*'Columbine' Bybloemen Breeder*

Darling, your encrypted coral
is wave and particle, wet
and dry. You are a creature
of the sea, plus its shell-like:
that old venetian paradox.

*'Julia Farnese' Rose Feathered*

You break with tradition,
expose what you wouldn't
even mention as flaws, delineate
your own *vade mecum,* risk
the interior, canyon and gorge.

*'Mabel' Flamed*

Cheeky, sticking out your bum,
knowing I'll chase you forever,
never catch up – licked
sherbet's tingle and fizz; chameleon
of blown, exploded glass.

*Tulip 'Red and Yellow'*

Your life as a parrot
is a sly disguise, utter nakedness;
raucous, a knack for tricks,
showing off, sudden flight.
Without you, I'm bereft.

*'James Wild' Feathered*

Neither vegetable nor fruit,
are you the devourer
or the devoured? No one
could be more open
without stumbling into dying.

*'Helen Josephine' Rose Breeder*

Given in to gravity, you
let yourself go – your widowed
grains of pollen, full stops
on thin air. I count six tongues,
nothing else to be mad about.

*'Dying Tulip 1'*

*Linda France*

## THE COLOURS MY MOTHER WORE

She wore the colours of these autumn trees
carnelians, agates, grandiose and subtle.
She blended them in paintings, tapestries,
of gardens, woods, perennially autumnal.

But when cataracts turned the tones too pale,
unknown to her, her flowers went florescent.
Then, when miniature work was bound to fail,
she took to painting liquid skies where pigment,

linseed oil, could blur of their own volition.
Skies hang silver -framed, windowed on my walls.
Live with a sunset, moon, a cloud formation

and soon they'll seem part of the furniture.
There's nothing new under the sky but palls
if we can't see its subtlety or grandeur.

*Mimi Khalvati*

## THE SPIRAL PAINTER

Now I wait for you in altered oils,
framed, unframed, a little dark and
rubbed around the edges; dressed,

undressed, I caress you with the
edge of my finger.

Now I animate you in arcadian reflections;
colour still holds me,
neither of us is lost.

Now I retouch everything. The stammer, the
sough, the bits no-one else can see; beyond the
yellow varnish of the horizon, the impossible sky.

*Chris Tutton*

## SARABANDE

In the rich sparseness
of late winter
time slows
to a lull going
nowhere, nearly

It is like a trance
induced by knowledge,
or an intimate love
always shadowed
by its counterpoint

Deep into summer
it will stay, this stopped
ground – as if leaves
could remain locked
in the sappy branches

Will stay as a dream
with nothing forgotten
even where the path
rises to sunlight
and airy silence

*Lawrence Sail*

*Sarabande: the fourth movement of the fourth of J.S. Bach's Suites for solo cello*

## STORIES

The ones she heard while she was drying her hair in front of the stove in the old farm kitchen. She never doubted that they were true. The chickens scratched around in the yard while she was scratching at the surface trying to understand the stories her mother harboured. She'd wake up in the night and rehearse one line she'd heard in the morning. She'd think about the day her grandfather died and she'd begged for more stories. She had her favourites of course. The one about the harvest moon and how it fades in the sky and the other that begins with a silence, a girl and then the cry of a bird. Now she craves more and more stories but they are all about words and seasons entwined with snow. She has no choice but to listen for its song.

*Wendy French*

## THE WOODCARVER

An old man is sitting by the Rialto.
He whittles at a figurine,
intricate fingers searching
for the human form
in the gnarl and knot of the seasons.

Each figurine becomes a languid adolescent,
a stretched uncluttered chord
placed once and left to sound
on a grand piano.

He died on a February night,
his stiff body propped on frosty cobbles.
They handled him like antique wood,
manoeuvring him onto a barge.

Then I found one floating. Quizzical,
she unnerves me with her doll's squint.
Washed of river slime, the little idol
is placed on my window sill.

Sometimes, on a windless dusk in autumn
when I open the casement,
she sings softly in Latin,
the pale notes moving like candlelight
out over the Laguna Morta to the dead.

*Andrew Nightingale*

## SWANSKIN

Sidney Nolan Trust – Printmaking

Today, this place is a smudge of charcoal
an etching on the blank, white page of the morning
or an indent on a sheet of Perspex.
*Intaglio, drypoint, collograph*
Your blood is ink, held in grooves,
your skin, dampened paper,
you're face down in the grass.

I'm a sketch made with a scalpel,
a sliver of cartridge paper.
My layers have been peeled back
peeled back
to reveal the soft white fibres of my life:

Our world is a smudge,
a possibility.
Not even a line of poetry,
Neither sentence nor phrase
As Berger once said,
*image before language.*

Our prints on paper
are synaptic flashes in the brain,
intaglio plates – projected onto
the inner retina,
(our third eye?)

This afternoon, *The Left Handers*
are writing and smudging
ink and charcoal
each has a black mark
down the length of their index fingers.
And the heat!

The heat is fizzing hummus
turning the tips of asparagus to mush,
souring the milk
baking the potato field bone-dry.
As I kneel down in the shade

to take a photograph,
I find a clump of dandelions.
*Dent de Lion,* lion's teeth.
This heat's hot enough to make a large cat pant.
This heat could scorch the throat,

reminds us of the rent
in the ozone layer,
that once wrapped the earth
like the swanskin from the printing press.
Somewhere beyond The Marches

in the distant belch of the city streets,
the hustle and hub-bub,
clouds of commuters' car fumes,
traffic slowing winding out of Birmingham.
But here the shadows

of the cherry trees
stripe the road,
fruit-pale yellow
and red,
clustering, ripening
in the late afternoon's doze.
There's a breeze now
and an old gate swings
open like a smile.

The sun's in my eyes
and my hat's pulled low.
Sweat's blooming behind
each knee.

A small-leaved lime tree
is humming with bees.

*Anne Caldwell*

## SELF MADE MAN

He picks his palette up, and starts to paint
Invests the canvas with expressive oils
The tight off-white stretched cloth absorbs the daubs
It's recognisable, sharp and severe
His brush fulfils its brief, portrays the traits
The early random-looking lines cohere
By increments an image constellates

My father's mother, as once drawn by him
in brown felt tip when I was in my teens
Beneath today's still life the play of genes
Beneath the leaf – the twig, the branch, the limb

He's traced me back, revealed the family tree
The embedded dna in dynasty

Next session's strokes will see this overlaid
With features I can claim as just my own
The part of me that passes for self-made
Fresh-grown from seeds so very long since sown
In quiet fields which never quite lay fallow
Which never quite wake up, nor ever sleep

Perhaps the me that's me is just skin deep

I hope he doesn't make me look too shallow

*Matt Harvey*

## SPOOKY POOKA'S MESSAGE TO THE NATION

*from an image by Spooky Pooka*

'Now let me tell you',
said the deer-headed man,
with twigs like dyspepsia
radiating from his stomach.

'Let me say
that in my time here,
with nothing for my naked pelvis
but these termite mounds,

I have found it
not as bad as it appears.
There is that hazel behind,
just waiting for April

and the other tree,
species still a mystery,
now a full six weeks
in gestation.

I wonder when the birth will be;
I believe it may be soon,
may be a time for joy,
may have colour in it'.

*Simon Williams*

## HELLIOGRAPHY

Smoke rises from the sheet. You angle your lens to focus the sun more powerfully, and etch the line of my nose into place: sculpting with light. The contours of my cheek, my brow, my chin, appear like fog on water. I watch with awe, and vow not to move while I serve as your model.

I observe you closer, perhaps, than I ought; with the right attention I believe I could be taught. Your finesse lights a blaze within me – envy and hunger in equal majesty.

Even my breaths are shallow, such is my effort not to alter my expression and reveal the tension playing out beneath my skin. The alchemy of your artistry provokes my hairs to stand erect – you draw light into shade, and shade into myself. I track the muscles of your back as you turn from me; inhale the lingering scent of lavender oil. A few more shifts of the lens and you stand aside, revealing the complete portrait.

But I look beyond the art to you, my artist. I note how your desire for greatness coils from you like smoke, and I wonder how best to concentrate that craving until it smoulders into flame.

*Judy Darley*

## FORGETFULNESS

We awake:
dog-eared, moth-bitten,
noctilucent clouds
still colouring
our blood.
Last night
we forgot things.
A man danced,
spoke in tongues
for his past,
babbled
something like love
and we sang
for his dance,
we sang with smoke,
with fire,
with forgetfulness.
We sang dry throated
and dreaming
through the witching hour…
Now, in the morning
our tongues smoulder
like the ashes
where we burnt
our little demons
on tiny slips of light

*Gaia Holmes*

## PURPLE HAZE

When Jimi glanced into his small attic mirror
while pouting his lips, unteasing his hair,
in a candle-like glint he saw George Frederic Handel
alarmingly wigless, alarmingly there.

'What have you been taking?' said Handel to Hendrix.
'Only the usual,' Jimi replied.
'I adore your high notes,' Handel whispered. 'But listen!
You cannot cheat sleep. I went blind when I tried.

Make friends with your sound man. Then fix the fuzz
pedal.
But discipline, boy! Cut your endless tracks short.'
Jimi shook is fine head. With no more breaths to meddle
George sank to roast chickens, his cellar of port.

*Alison Brackenbury*

## VENUS ON MARS

*after Botticelli*

He'd excited her at first; in fact
they'd had stars named after each other
as gifts. Lucky they decided on that
rather than the tattoos.

She faked it again this afternoon –
not that he'd notice. If only
those horny little satyrs
would scarper she could sneak off.

That guy who whizzed by earlier
chasing a huge black boar into those woods
– now he was constellation material,
pure and simple. And anyway,

she'd definitely gone off the kind of men
who feel the need to shave beyond
their chins.

*Kathryn Daszkievicz*

## NEW YORK HOTEL

In the lobby by the revolving glass doors was an old man dressed like Gene Kelly and crooning 'Singing in the Rain' without any musical accompaniment. His voice was frail, but this only served to give the song an added poignancy Yet no one stopped to listen, or to watch his surprisingly deft tap dance.

After dropping a couple of coins into a hat at the end of the song, I asked him why he was doing this. He told me he had come to the city to look for work more than fifty years ago. While waiting in the lobby by these same doors to speak to someone about a job as a porter, he had started singing popular songs of the day to himself. The hotel owner had happened to pass by in that moment.

'You've got a great voice, kid,' the owner said, taking a puff on his cigar. 'I'll pay you a dollar a day just to stand here and do what you're doing now.'

That old owner was long since dead and the pay had never gone above a dollar a day. Nevertheless, with leftover food from the kitchen, an attic room in the hotel, and with a few tips, he got by.

I wondered why with such a voice he had never tried his hand at getting a record deal.

'I often thought of it,' he said, 'but at first I was afraid of appearing ungrateful to the man who offered me this work when I was down on my luck. Then the years passed more quickly than I thought they would. Now I have no choice except to keep singing here until I'm done. And now if you will excuse me...'

He cleared his throat, spread his arms, and gave everything he had to another song no one had time to listen to.

*Ian Seed*

## THE GESTURE

To step forward to the canvas then back from it
without making a mark, and to do this
again and again as the paint on the brush
thickens, as my eye, my hand, my heart
refuse to repeat the gesture once made freely
with a synthesis of joy. What Auerbach called
the safety net of manner could be mine
if I admitted it, to break my fall and rest there
saved by repetition. What you might say
is 'Nobody paints like him, amazingly prolific
for his age, such energy, such vision', easy words
like that, but exactly so, I should indeed
be nobody with nothing left to show but a blank
and vacuous deception. No, I'm not ready yet.

*John Mole*

## POSTCOLONIAL

There is a certain kind of Englishman
who will adopt your country.
He'll know it better than you do.
He'll even speak the language, if imperfectly.
He'll go to parties with all the 'in' people.
Soon, he'll be advising ministers on Peace, War and
Poverty,
before sailing down the Río Magdalena
escorted by the FARC.
He'll visit cocaine labs and the best hotels.
First and foremost, he's an amateur, an enthusiast,
bred on the playing fields of Wellington and
Winchester.
He'll return with his loot of film and tales,
dine out on them for years.
But there's one thing that has him flummoxed
(and I've a soft spot for this Englishman).
For the life of him, he can't dance.

*Isabel Bermudez*

## CUTTING IN

It's hard to know where to begin
all things being already in progress
the painting already alive before the first brush
is dipped before the first colour is mixed
from the marigolds lilacs poppies long after
they have lived long after the teenage gardener
sowed their seeds in the run-down remnants
of what his grandfather called the family home

– but whose story is this that insists
its well into the canvas woven by the girl
in the tenth district while his seed rounded
her belly as she rounded into womanhood
and he in exploration of what it is to be he
steps back already proud of his work?

*Anne Stewart*

## NANCY'S STAR TURN

We were five years old, newly-fledged to school
shy, except for one girl with pretty yellow curls

who spoke loudly and cheerfully in a strange
accent, didn't defer to teachers or avoid the boys,

but when we gathered to drink our third of a pint
of milk at break time, climbed onto a desk

(it wasn't even her desk), and raising her squeaky
voice in a shrill rendering of *Nelly the Elephant,*

proceeded to click and tap the heels
of her impossibly shiny patent leather shoes

in a dance whose fierce percussive beat
thrilled our innocence, suggesting there were worlds

wider and more exciting than our own,
of which Nancy knew but we could only dream.

*Alwyn Marriage*

## CHIFFON
*Consett, c1970*

Miss Maddison, with her stick, and haematite-red
lipstick,
Barks orders in time with a brisk mazurka. *Fifth
position!*
Seventeen little girls lined up in the steel-town drill-hall
Flash their *grand battements* to their own reflection.

Dust pirouettes in the dingy light. Stale sweat on satin
And crêpe-de-chine. Blurred windows to a distant world,
Yellowing in Woolworth's frames in the changing-room,
Sleazy and glamorous, Degas' poor shivering girls

Stretch and yawn in pink chiffon. He scares us a little,
The cadaverous pianist, old and slow. He is a tortoise.
Almost dead.
He clanks the keys like a stick on the cemetery railings.
It is winter. At the end of the street, the engine sheds

Squat beneath batteries. High priests of the cooling
towers
Scowl down on tight-lipped ranks of coal-holes, chimney
stacks. They glare
Over the rain-hammered fell for miles. Masonic
mysteries.
A glamour we have yet to grow into splutters and flares.

If we *étendue* high enough, girls, we can *sauté* right out
of here…
Sinter and rough ore, coke and flux. Wild
transmutations,
Inscrutable, sulphurous, raked from Earth's guts,
overshadowing us.
Strange lights from dark furnaces. Billows of choking
pink chiffon.

*Katrina Porteous*

## THE HOUSE OF DANCING CACTI

On Saturday nights
the squat mammilarias
and the leggy saguaros
heft themselves,
and their earth-filled pots,
from the shelves
and tables,
gather on the sofa
in one prickly mass
to watch
*Strictly Come Dancing.*

They love the sparkling,
the jaunty trotting,
the little kisses and hisses
of dancing shoes
on the glossy floors.

If you listen carefully
you might hear them
sighing after watching
a dexterous loop or lift.
Treasure this.
The sigh of a cactus
is a rare and precious thing
that may, one day, save you.

Mostly the house
is still and dry
but some days
a rich sirocco wind
swirls through its rooms
splaying books,
ruching rugs, ruffling cats
and the cacti wobble and spin
to the round music
of their homeland
as they remember the heat,
the sharp nights pricked with stars,
their succulent bodies
full of juice,
ready to quench the dawn.

*Gaia Holmes*

## NIDDERDALE

Alice made a nest of coats in the caravan she borrowed from a friend. She was off grid. It rained all night. Nidderdale rain, heavy and persistent, drumming on the metal roof of her box-shaped room, with the sound of the river like a bass note in the music of water. Her father would have remarked, it's raining stair-rods, lass or raining cats and dogs. She thought of Escher's stairways leading nowhere, the Bourgeois print of a woman cradling an angry baby at the bottom of a flight of steps. At night she dreamt of stray terriers falling from the sky. Would she be furred-in, rather than snowed in? Limp, sodden bodies piled up against the cinder blocks of the caravan? Waking to sunshine was a relief. She parted the yellow beaded curtain and looked up to the grit-stone moors, birch trees shimmering like unspoken words…

*Anne Caldwell*

## SENTENCES FOR VIVALDI'S *GLORIA*

*[following No.3, Laudamus te]*

In the salt brightness of the lagoon, glory
In the worn cities and the hills, praise
In the local weather of love, adoration
In heart and mind, the working muscle of thankfulness

*[following No.7, Domini fili]*

In the slow hours of reckoning, pain
In time, the sense of time misjudged
In riches locked away, the failure of love
In every war, the simple cruelty of the strong

*[following No.10, Qui sedes ad dexteram]*

In help and laughter, a grounded hope
In spite of nightmares, the dream of grace
In singers' exposed voices, trust
In the pulse of music, the quickening trumpets of glory

*Lawrence Sail*

## BIRD OF THE SEA

*after a stone carving by Bridget McCrum*

remember
her like
the font
that was leaking
the water
that held
the first flight

she is all of the egg
the shell
the white
the yolk

she is all of the nest
the branch
the tree
the shelter

there on
the ground
she writhes
like a sea
serpent
tarred and feathered

she is all of the pain
of earth
of rock
of sky

she is all of the light
of union
of moon
of metal

*Susan Taylor*

## ALLEGORY OF WINTER

*after the painting by Remedios Varo*

*You've imprisoned us.*

Dear birds,
I promise you won't die.
You won't starve.
I'm protecting you
from winter's assault.

*We don't always starve*
*in the cold months.*

You look so spring-like
in your transparent
diamond casings.
How exquisite you all are,
so bright and various,
each of you an artist.
Each of you poised
on the brink of flight.

*We're sealed off,*
*can only glimpse each other.*
*The enormous snowflakes*
*are blue with cold,*
*the sky is grey-indigo.*
*The branchless trees*
*have deep whorls*

*and the gashing spines*
*of giant brown cacti.*
*They bend towards us like humans.*
*Release us, we beg you*
*into actual spring.*

I can't quite hear you.

*We're muffled*
*beyond endurance.*

I too despair that beauty
should be so confined.
Hold your breath.
Forgive me
for taking you by surprise.
It's winter – a savage time.
Can you bear it?

*Moniza Alvi*

## UNDERGROUND CABARET

The steep stone steps led down to a restaurant in a cellar with long wooden tables and shelves stacked with dusty bottles of wine. Each evening a different dish was prepared, but only in limited quantities, and I wondered if I had arrived too late. I was the last customer to be allowed in.

At the end of the meal, straws were drawn to decide which one of us would perform that evening. It seemed inevitable the straw would come to me.

I took off my shirt and announced that with the point of my steak knife I would incise the story of the day into my skin, and then sing the events depicted there with improvised lyrics.

It was bound to be a distortion of the truth, but I hoped to make it seem authentic, not only for the sake of my reputation, but also in order not to break the spell of the stories which my audience told themselves to make their own lives real.

*Ian Seed*

## THE ARTIST'S HAND

*on the death of Barbara Hepworth*

The hand she had cast in bronze
was her thinking hand. Its rhythms
passed through tools and into stone.

She said this left hand was her listening hand
It heard the flaws beneath those surfaces
she worked before her eyes could see.

When she was young a palmist
read this hand, but then refused to tell
what she saw etched there.

Did she see deft flames curl
round upright forms? Smoke coil
through perfect holes in scented guarea wood?

Smoke that would silence hands
which thought and heard. Smoke
the colour of stone from Hopton Wood.

*Kathryn Daszkievicz*

## OUTPATIENTS

In Cardiology, the corridor
is a bright blue stream of lino, a river
where, lined up like fishermen on a shore,
patients face patients ranged along the other.

One old fisherman, bent over his cane,
sings quietly to himself. A farawayness
surfaces like a shoal; a swirling chain
of choruses he strums like Orpheus.

Weddings, celebrations, birthdays, now quicken,
now subside, as his voice gets louder, softer,
drifts down 'the narrows of the Arda River'.

*Ali Kemal Ali!* they call. Remember
Ali Kemal? – that murdered politician
who was Boris Johnson's great-grandfather?

*Mimi Khalvati*

# A PALMFUL OF RAIN

Rain. July so far as wet as June. In the courtyard a family of bluetits flits through the seeding cranesbill twitteringly, like a handful of seedheads themselves. I park by the little churchyard with its old wooden gate, lichen-bearded. They've taken the two condemned but as far as I could see perfectly healthy young trees, and the meadow is marked by two absences. Behind, in the cemetery, in rain, beneath reprieved trees, someone is hunched on a bench in front of the graves. I can see even from here how he's brushing water from his face. With a now-familiar shock I remember yet again that my mother is dead

I tilt my face to the rain, hold up my palms, think about absence, about washing-away. And then the dance. T makes the shapes of tai chi. J smiles serenely. A is a mad monk then a Sufi dervish. I forget death, absence, illness, stress – I forget who I am in the dance. There is a moment when the music and my body slip me, whoever 'me' is, through a narrow keyhole into ecstasy. Time starts to slide and I'm back on the blue heights of Treshnish, above the white crescent of Traigh Calgaraidh, wind roaring at my ears until all thought is washed out and the wind is me and I am the wind

and again there is only the dance

*Roselle Angwin*

## MAYA

*after Rabindranath Tagore*

Lady, your tresses fly in the sun:
strong spider webs sporting honey-dew.
Free and boundless are your raven locks,
but their roots are grounded in your head.

Lady, your sari floats in the sun:
gossamer fishnets you cast adrift.
Light and shade, bright dawn and secret night,
play seek and hide in your timeless bliss.

Lady, your figure swirls in the sun:
dervish dancing to a divine drum.
You are also She who is implored;
you are the world's rhythm and heartbeat.

Lady, your arms stretch to hold the sun:
a posture of maternal embrace.
Your every move is celebration.
You are Maya, my playful Mother.

*Debjani Chatterjee*

## DUTCH STILL LIFE

What if when looking at three eggs
resting on a table one rolls and hits the floor
there is no sound for while the yolk swirls round
the fragility of eggs is never doubted
and what if at that moment the hanging pheasant
breaks loose his cord and flies squawking to be free
from the confines of paintings and then again, what if
the maid filling the water jug is you,

not sure of who you are, or who you're meant to be
and if upstairs there are those who break the bread,
eat it with relish, wiping their mouths, so sure
of their presence in the dining scene, who never find
a need to wonder will there be bread tomorrow who will
still be fed?

*Wendy French*

## THREE PAINTED STORKS

Every morning since, you wake exhausted to a muddled
barrage
of images and sounds, impressions, photographs you
took or missed,
the cacophony of city traffic and street-sellers, the
insistent hands-out
'Please' of children being trained to beg for life, and
peacocks
and monkeys' tiger-warning cries at Ranthambore, and
cattle snuffling
in village roadside litter piles, the raucous horns of
traffic on the highways…

except on the mornings of the painted storks in Agra.
Those days,
you wake to heart-rise, the silent seeing again of that
painted sky as –

sitting low on a courtyard wall of Emperor Akbar's Fort,
already
suffused with its red sandstone glow, already
overwhelmed
by the Mughals' admiration of beauty: The Pearl
Mosque,
the Golden Pavilion, the Sheesh Mahal's shining glass
mosaic,

every surface intricate, cut or inlaid, embossed or etched,
painted in vibrant colour or powdered gem or plain pure
gold –
you watch a last hint of cotton cloud disappear behind
the Baby Taj
and the sky, no taint of Delhi's grey, spreads over your
head in infinite blue.

And it's this magnificent creation, this vast translucent
wash stretched
thin, horizon to horizon, that you're admiring, already
hardly able to bear
the beauty of it, when three painted storks stream across
the sky –
too high to see their colour, their long orange beaks, their
pink flesh –
just three black arrows, spindle legs trailing pencil-
straight
to end in the compact 'V' of the black tips of their feet…

as though it were possible… as though the Shah himself
had returned
to perfect his design, to order his final decorative touch.

*Anne Stewart*

## INGRAINED

I've met the sand of this beach
more than once.
This grain underfoot was a shell
I held to your ear;
this, the blade of scapula
from the wing of a gull
whose call made us startle
then laugh;
this particle lodged beneath
my fingernail;
lost itself in our sheets
for a time.
And this one, this speck,
in the fragment
of a star
whose light danced
from your eyes to mine.

*Judy Darley*

## SYMPHONY

Thunder plays a piano
piece for left hand, cello

storms after woodwind in a
penguin suit sky.

Moonlight intermezzo
melts into first quiet

chords of daybreak,
shimmering like

young leaves on
branches arced with rain.

*Chris Tutton*

## ACKNOWLEDGEMENTS


'Allegory of Winter' by Moniza Alvi from "Blackbird Bye Bye" Bloodaxe Books (2018) Reproduced with permission of Bloodaxe Books. 'Cello Suites' by Roselle Angwin from "Looking for Icarus" (Bluechrome).

'Keelby, 1966' by Alison Brackenbury published in "Stand Magazine", 'Sheela na gig, St Michaels, Oxford' by Alison Brackenbury, published in "Poetry Review".

'Nidderdale' by Anne Caldwell has appeared in "Valley Press Anthology of Yorkshire Poetry", Valley Press 2018. 'Adoration of the Kings' by Martyn Crucefix forthcoming from "Agenda".

'Lytton' by Kathryn Daszkievicz published in "Tears in the Fence", 'Venus on Mars' by Kathryn Daszkievicz published in "Dream Catcher".

'Wild Garlic' by Mark Gwynne Jones from "Psychicbread" (Route 2003) A musical rendition of 'Wild Garlic' appeared on the CD "In the Light of This" (Route 2006)

'Background Music' by Mimi Khalvati published in the "Long Poem Magazine" 'The Artist as a Child' by Mimi Khalvati published in "Smoke" 'Outpatients' by Mimi Khalvati published in "Poem International"

'Nancy's Star Turn' by Alwyn Marriage published in "Nancy's Star Turn" in Project Boast Anthology 2018. 'The Song' by John Mole and 'The Gesture' by John Mole published in "Gestures and Counterpoints" (Shoestring Press 2017).

'The Woodcarver' by Andrew Nightingale from "The Big Wheel" (Oversteps Books; www.overstepsbooks.com)

'Sarabande' and 'Sentences for Vivaldi's *Gloria*' by Lawrence Sail to be published in "Guises" by Bloodaxe Books 2020.'Underground Cabaret' by Ian Seed first published in "Tears in the Fence", 'New York Hotel' by Ian Seed from "New York Hotel" Shearsman 2018.

'The Insoluble Harmonies of Colour' by Chris Tutton from "Angles of Repose", Avalanche Books 2012, 'The Ghost Dance' by Chris Tutton and 'The Spiral Painter' by Chris Tutton from "Impossible Memories", Avalanche Books (2016) 'Symphony' by Chris Tutton from "Seasons of Winter", Avalanche Books 2005.

'Ophelia Drowning in the Tate' by Simon Williams from "Quinks" (Oversteps Books 2006)